PRAIRIE DOG SONG

The Key to Saving
North America's Grasslands

by **Susan L. Roth** and **Cindy Trumbore**

collages by **Susan L. Roth**

Lee & Low Books Inc.
New York

For Alex and Dana, with love —*S.L.R.*
To the memory of Karl Baymor —*C.T.*

Acknowledgments
Grateful thanks go to Dr. Gerardo Ceballos for his expert
reading of the manuscript, and to Laura Paulson of The
Nature Conservancy, Dr. Nélida Barajas, and Dr. Rurik List
for helping the authors ensure accuracy. Thanks also go
to Judy Calman and Nathan Newcomer of the New Mexico
Wilderness Alliance and Mark Hakkila of the Bureau of Land
Management, Las Cruces District Office, for providing us
with advice on exploring the grasslands of Otero Mesa in
New Mexico. S.L.R. adds special thanks to Nancy Patz for her
generous help with this book; to Harry Trumbore, Sharon
Cresswell, and Olga Guartan; and, as always, to JR et al.

Book design by Christy Hale
Book production by The Kids at Our House
The text is set in Rockwell
The illustrations are rendered in paper and fabric collage
Manufactured in China by Jade Productions, January 2016
Printed on paper from responsible sources
10 9 8 7 6 5 4 3 2 1
First Edition
Library of Congress Cataloging-in-Publication Data
Roth, Susan L., author, illustrator.
Prairie dog song : the key to saving North America's grasslands / by
Susan L. Roth and Cindy Trumbore ; collages by Susan L. Roth. — First
edition.   pages cm
Summary: "Cumulative text based on an old folksong alternating with
additional scientific information explores the role of prairie dogs, a
keystone species in North America's grasslands, and conservation
efforts to restore the balance of plants and animals of the Janos, Mexico,
prairie dog complex. Backmatter includes timeline, photographs,
music, prairie dog facts, glossary, and authors' sources"—Provided
by publisher.
Audience: Ages 6–10
ISBN 978-1-62014-245-5 (hardcover : alk. paper)
1. Prairie dogs—Juvenile literature. 2. Grassland ecology—Juvenile
literature. 3. Grassland animals—Juvenile literature. 4. Children's songs—
Texts. I. Trumbore, Cindy, author. II. Title.
QL737.R68R67 2016   599.36'7—dc23   2015025915

This is a book about a furry animal called a prairie dog.

Part of the book is a song.

You may sing the song or just say the words.

If you would like to sing the song, the music is in the back of the book.

There were some holes
In the middle of the ground,
The prettiest holes
That you ever did see.
And the grasses waved
All around, all around,
And the grasses waved all around.

Once grasses waved like a green-and-gold sea over North America.

The land where the grasses grew had been shaped long ago by glaciers, giant walls of moving ice. The glaciers crept over the central part of the continent, flattening the land before melting away.

Lying in the shadow of the Rocky Mountains, the flat land did not get much rain. Trees could not grow there easily, but different kinds of grass could. By ten thousand years ago, grasslands stretched from southern Canada all the way to northern Mexico.

Billions of prairie dogs, furry animals that are a kind of squirrel, lived in the grass. Short mounds of dirt marked the entrance holes to their burrows underground. The mounds were like watching posts. The prairie dogs stood up on the dirt to search for enemies.

And down these holes
Lived prairie dogs,
With the friskiest pups
That you ever did see.
Yes, the prairie dogs built
Their homes in the ground.
And the grasses waved
All around, all around,
And the grasses waved all around.

Prairie dogs still live in parts of North America. There are five different species. They live in flat, rolling prairies and in drier desert lands.

The most common species is the black-tailed prairie dog, which uses its long front claws to dig tunnels underground. These tunnels connect to a maze of rooms. Some rooms are for listening for predators, enemies that eat prairie dogs. Other rooms are used for sleeping, storing food, and raising playful prairie dog pups. Another room is a toilet area.

As they build their tunnels, prairie dogs help the grass grow. Like big earthworms, they loosen the soil when they dig. They make the soil richer by mixing in dead plants and animal waste. Their digging also makes small holes that trap water in the dirt. More plants, and more kinds of plants, can grow in this moist, loose, rich soil.

And side by side
Were burrowing owls,
The littlest owls
That you ever did see.
Yes, the burrowing owls
They borrowed burrows.
And the prairie dogs built
Their homes in the ground.
And the grasses waved
All around, all around,
And the grasses waved all around.

Many animals share prairie dog burrows. Snakes and spiders live right in the burrows prairie dogs are using. Tiny burrowing owls make their homes in old, empty burrows. Inside, the owls build nests of dried manure. The manure helps hide the owls' smell and attracts a kind of beetle that the owls eat. Each spring, burrowing owls raise their newborn owlets in these nests.

And up above
Some bison grazed,
With the heaviest hooves
That you ever did see.
Yes, the bison grazed
And stomped their hooves.
And the owls burrowed,
And the prairie dogs built
Their homes in the ground.
And the grasses waved
All around, all around,
And the grasses waved all around.

Prairie dogs and bison both lived in grasslands long ago and can still be found together in some places. The animals help each other survive, and they help the grass too.

Prairie dogs nibble the leaves of some plants, letting other leaves take in light and water. They also nibble the different grasses, causing them to take up more nitrogen from the soil. Nitrogen is a nutrient that helps plants grow.

The bison eat the healthy plants and nitrogen-rich grasses. They graze tall plants down to the ground, creating areas with low grass. Then prairie dogs, which need low grass to see their predators, can move in.

As the bison walk over the land, their heavy hooves break up the dirt. The loose soil lets more seeds grow into grasses for the prairie dogs to eat.

And overhead
There flew some birds,
The biggest birds
That you ever did see.
Yes, the big birds soared,
So the prairie dogs barked.
And the bison grazed,
And the owls burrowed,
And the prairie dogs built
Their homes in the ground.
And the grasses waved
All around, all around,
And the grasses waved all around.

When golden eagles nest near prairie dogs, the prairie dogs make up at least half of the eagles' diet. So prairie dogs are constantly alert for golden eagles and other predators. The prairie dogs stand on their mounds, watching the horizon. They have a complex warning system that includes barking "Chee-chee, chee-chee!" over and over. The bark describes the exact kind of enemy to other prairie dogs.

Golden eagles are named for the gold-colored feathers on their heads and necks. These huge, swift birds are among the largest and fastest birds of prey in North America. Their wingspan stretches up to 7 feet (2.1 meters) across. When the eagles spot animals they want to eat, they can dive at speeds faster than a roller coaster can travel.

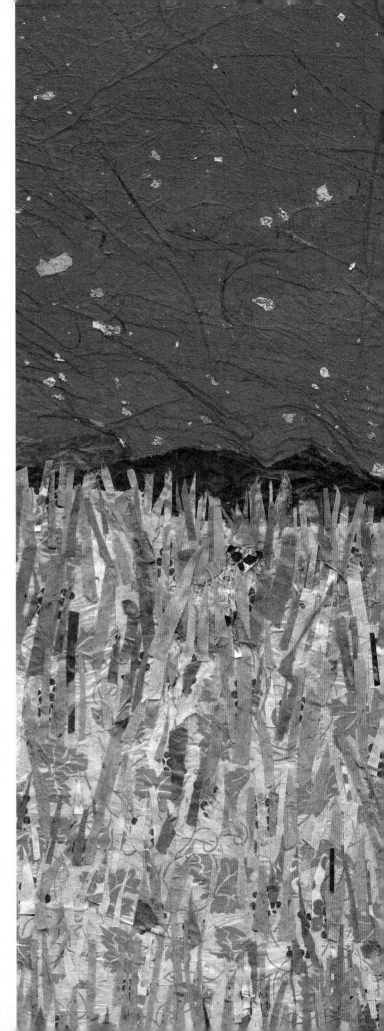

And in the night
There crept some ferrets,
On the softest feet
That you ever did see.
Yes, the ferrets crept,
So the prairie dogs hid.
And the big birds soared,
And the bison grazed,
And the owls burrowed,
And the prairie dogs built
Their homes in the ground.
And the grasses waved
All around, all around,
And the grasses waved all around.

Black-footed ferrets, a kind of weasel, eat almost nothing except prairie dogs. When ferrets slip into prairie dog burrows, they feed on the prairie dogs and then stay there to eat, sleep, and raise their own young.

Prairie dogs can fight back. If ferrets enter their burrows, the prairie dogs pile dirt over the entrances to trap the ferrets inside.

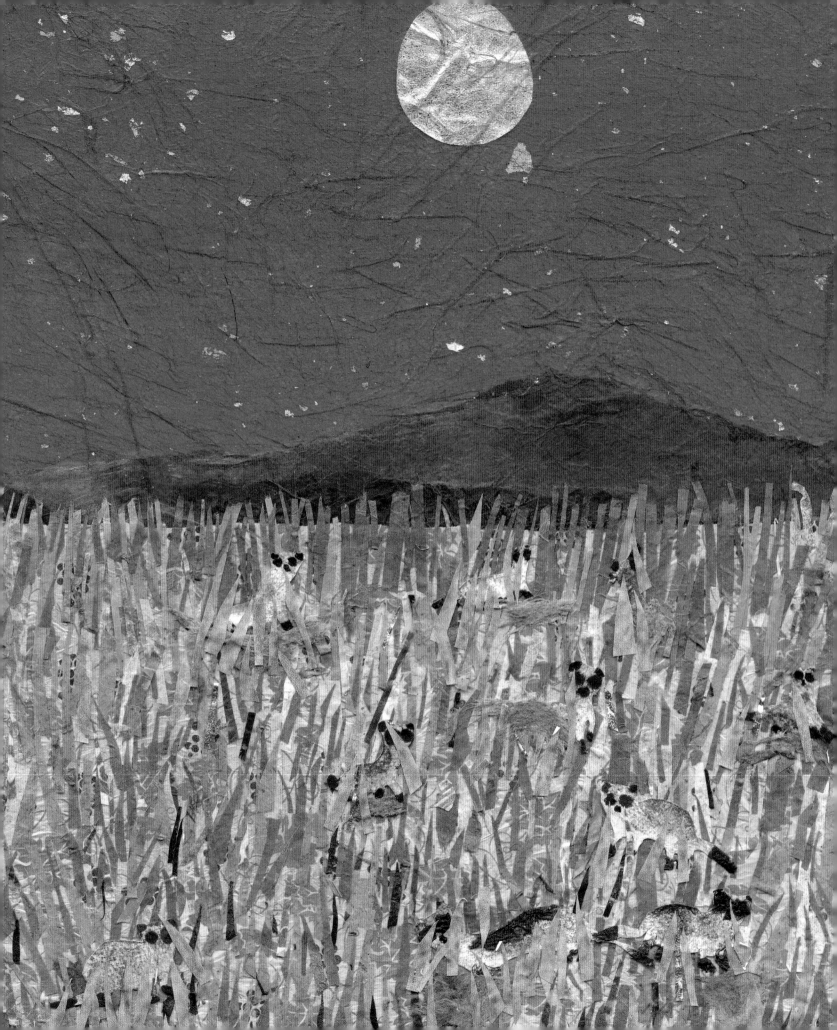

And then one year
Came ranchers and farmers,
With the fattest cows
That you ever did see.
Yes, ranches and farms
They covered the grass
Where the ferrets crept,
And the big birds soared,
And the bison grazed,
And the owls burrowed,
And the prairie dogs built
Their homes in the ground.
And the grasses waved
Here and there, here and there,
And the grasses waved here and there.

For thousands of years, prairie dogs lived alongside the Native peoples of the grasslands. Some Native groups survived by gathering plants and hunting the big animals, including bison, that ate the rich grass near prairie dogs' burrows. Other groups were both hunters and farmers, growing crops such as corn, beans, and squash.

Then, in the 1800s, the United States government began forcing Native peoples from the grasslands so the land could be offered to settlers. The settlers saw fine, fertile areas where they could graze their cattle and horses and grow crops. They covered the land with fields, ranches, houses, and roads that destroyed the prairie dogs' territory.

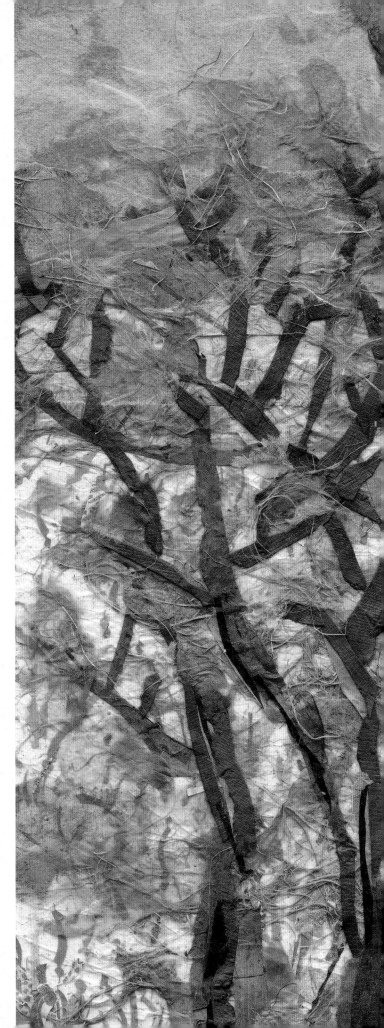

And over time
Mesquite moved in,
With the longest roots
That you ever did see.
Yes, the deep tree roots
Sucked up the water
Where the ferrets crept,
And the big birds soared,
And the bison grazed,
And the owls burrowed,
And the prairie dogs built
Their homes in the ground.
And the grasslands turned
Into desert land,
And the grass turned to desert land.

Within sixty years of the arrival of farmers and
ranchers, most of the prairie dogs were dead.
The settlers did not understand the role prairie
dogs played in keeping the grasses healthy. They
believed that prairie dogs ate the grass meant
for their cows and horses. The settlers were also
afraid their animals would step in prairie dog holes
and break their legs. So people put poison in the
prairie dogs' burrows, which also killed the other
animals living there.

Prairie dogs, the animals that ate them, and the
animals that lived with them began to disappear.
So did the bison, which were hunted for their skins.
Then mesquite, a tree with long, snaky roots that
suck up water from the ground, spread over the
grasslands. Prairie dogs chew up mesquite roots
to destroy the plant, which blocks their view of
predators. Now there were fewer prairie dogs to
control the mesquite and dig holes that trap water
in the soil. The grasslands turned into desert land.

But in one place
Lived prairie dogs,
'Cause ranchers and farmers
Left the burrows alone.
Yes, the bison were gone,
And the ferrets too.
But the big birds soared,
And the owls burrowed,
And the prairie dogs built
Their homes in the ground.
And the grasses waved
All around, all around,
And the grasses waved all around.

In a place called Janos, in northern Mexico, black-tailed prairie dogs still live, play, and search for food. Electricity did not come to this part of the world until the late 1990s. Local ranchers and farmers had mostly been using old-fashioned equipment and techniques that did not hurt the land as much as more modern methods.

A group of connected black-tailed prairie dog burrows is called a town, and a group of towns close enough to be visited by one black-footed ferret is called a complex. The Janos prairie dog complex was once the largest in North America, covering an area of about 212 square miles (549 square kilometers). Today it is about one-fourth that size.

And in that place
Some people saw
More prairie dogs
Than you ever did see.
Yes, the people said,
"Let's save this place."
And the big birds soared,
And the owls burrowed,
And the prairie dogs built
Their homes in the ground.
And the grasses waved
All around, all around,
And the grasses waved all around.

In 1988, Gerardo Ceballos, an environmental scientist, was driving from the southwestern United States to Mexico. As he passed through the desert in Janos, he came upon grasses waving, prairie dogs barking, burrowing owls perching on mounds, and golden eagles soaring. He began researching prairie dogs and found that they are a keystone species—animals that, through their activities, help many plants and other animals survive.

All the plants and animals that live together in a place, along with nonliving things such as sunlight and water, make up an ecosystem. If a keystone species disappears from an ecosystem, the plants and animals that depend on the keystone species disappear too.

And then one night
There came some ferrets,
The ones that crept
On the softest feet.
Yes, the people brought
The ferrets back.
And the ferrets crept,
And the big birds soared,
And the owls burrowed,
And the prairie dogs built
Their homes in the ground.
And the grasses waved
All around, all around,
And the grasses waved all around.

Dr. Ceballos and other scientists began working to preserve the Janos grasslands. They decided that to make the area completely healthy again, they should try to restore the same balance of plants and animals that it had before humans disturbed the land. They started with black-footed ferrets, which were making a comeback thanks to a United States government captive breeding program. In 2001, ninety-one ferrets from the program were released into the Janos prairie dog town.

One of the first released ferrets was not sure what to do when its cage door was opened, even though it had been trained to enter a prairie dog tunnel. So a scientist lifted the training tube with the ferret inside and put it right in front of a burrow. Ferrets are curious, and this one did what ferrets are supposed to do. It crawled down into the burrow.

And then one day
There came some bison,
The ones that grazed
And stomped their hooves.
Yes, the people brought back
Bison too.
And the bison grazed,
And the ferrets crept,
And the big birds soared,
And the owls burrowed . . .

In 2005, The Nature Conservancy, an organization that works to protect nature around the world, bought the huge cattle ranch within the Janos prairie dog complex. Reserva Rancho El Uno (El Uno Ranch Reserve) would be a place to save and recover animals that had once lived in this part of Mexico.

Many Conservancy staff and scientists began working to make their vision for Rancho El Uno come true. One day, the project's coordinator, Nélida Barajas, talked about the ranch with her friend Rurik List, a scientist who was studying the prairie dogs. He said, "*Necesitamos bisontes.*" ("We need bison.")

Bison were once a big part of the culture of Janos. The elders of the community could remember herds of bison running in the grasslands. So The Nature Conservancy began to work with other groups to bring back the bison. In November 2009, twenty-three bison from a park in South Dakota were released into the Janos grasslands under the care of Rancho El Uno.

Local ranchers could see that the bison were good for the grass. The bison don't just break up the dirt. They play and roll in it, carving out pools that trap rainwater and help the grass grow.

And the prairie dogs built
Their homes in the ground. . . .

Just ten days after the bison arrived, the work of everyone who was trying to protect the Janos grasslands was rewarded. The president of Mexico declared that the entire grasslands, which included Rancho El Uno, were now the Janos Biosphere Reserve (JBR). The JBR was the first native grassland ecosystem to be protected by the federal government of Mexico.

The staff at Rancho El Uno are dedicated to helping the local ranchers use grazing practices that are better for the land. A group of ranchers now raises smaller herds of cows and allows the grass to recover after the cattle have grazed on it.

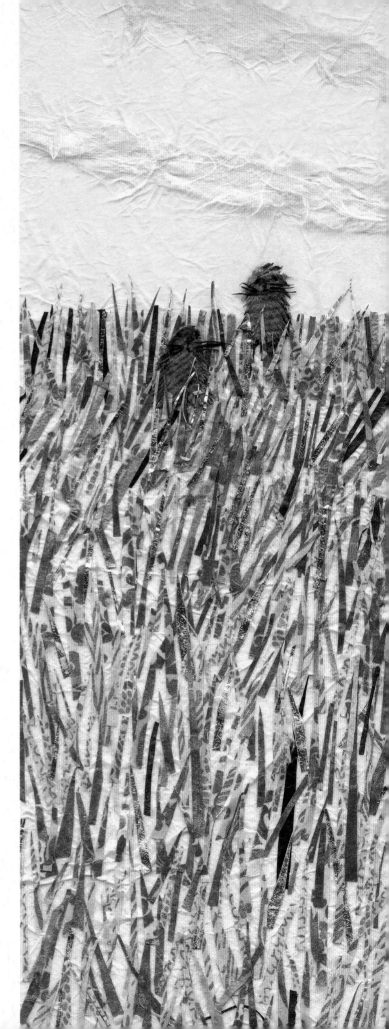

And the prairie dogs jumped
And yipped, "*WEE-OO!*"
And the grasses waved
All around, all around,
And the grasses waved all around.

As black-tailed prairie dogs scan the horizon for predators, one will often jump up, throw its front paws in the air, and yip, "Wee-oo!" One after another, more prairie dogs jump up and yip. Then the first jump-yipper starts to hunt for grass and seeds to eat. It knows that its neighbors are alert and watching out for its survival.

The people at Rancho El Uno are watching out for prairie dogs too. They want everyone to know how important the prairie dogs are. So they invite people of all ages to visit the ranch to see the bison, the precious grasslands, and the prairie dogs that help the green and gold grasses grow.

Prairie Dog Song

arranged by **Dale Trumbore**

The tune and form of the song in this book are based on a very old folk song known as "The Green Grass Grows All Around" or "The Green Grass Grew All Around." There are several versions of this song. The earliest is probably an Irish song called "The Rattling Bog," which has been dated to 1877. A version called "The Everlasting Circle" was collected in Cornwall, England, in 1905. A 1909 publication describes the song as using the "piling up" method of songwriting. As each new idea is introduced, the singer repeats the ideas that went before, making them "pile up" on one another.

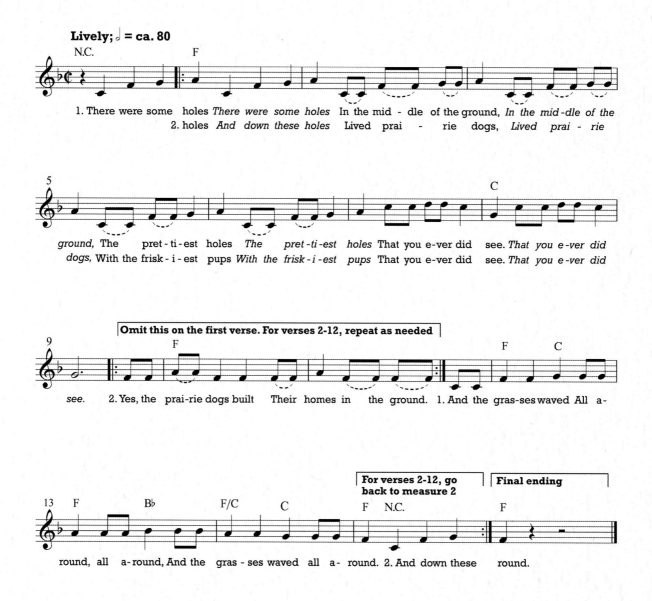

3. And side by side
   Were burrowing owls,
   The littlest owls
   That you ever did see.
   Yes, the burrowing owls
   They borrowed burrows.
   And the prairie dogs built
   Their homes in the ground.
   [Refrain 1]
   And the grasses waved
   All around, all around,
   And the grasses waved all around.

4. And up above
   Some bison grazed,
   With the heaviest hooves
   That you ever did see.
   Yes, the bison grazed
   And stomped their hooves.
   And the owls burrowed,
   And the prairie dogs built
   Their homes in the ground.
   [Refrain 1]

5. And overhead
   There flew some birds,
   The biggest birds
   That you ever did see.
   Yes, the big birds soared,
   So the prairie dogs barked.
   And the bison grazed,
   And the owls burrowed,
   And the prairie dogs built
   Their homes in the ground.
   [Refrain 1]

6. And in the night
   There crept some ferrets,
   On the softest feet
   That you ever did see.
   Yes, the ferrets crept,
   So the prairie dogs hid.
   And the big birds soared,
   And the bison grazed,
   And the owls burrowed,
   And the prairie dogs built
   Their homes in the ground.
   [Refrain 1]

7. And then one year
   Came ranchers and farmers,
   With the fattest cows
   That you ever did see.
   Yes, ranches and farms
   They covered the grass
   Where the ferrets crept,
   And the big birds soared,
   And the bison grazed,
   And the owls burrowed,
   And the prairie dogs built
   Their homes in the ground.
   [Refrain 2]
   And the grasses waved
   Here and there, here and there,
   And the grasses waved here and there.

8. And over time
   Mesquite moved in,
   With the longest roots
   That you ever did see.
   Yes, the deep tree roots
   Sucked up the water
   Where the ferrets crept,
   And the big birds soared,
   And the bison grazed,
   And the owls burrowed,
   And the prairie dogs built
   Their homes in the ground.
   [Refrain 3]
   And the grasslands turned
   Into desert land,
   And the grass turned to desert land.

9. But in one place
   Lived prairie dogs,
   'Cause ranchers and farmers
   Left the burrows alone.
   Yes, the bison were gone,
   And the ferrets too.
   But the big birds soared,
   And the owls burrowed,
   And the prairie dogs built
   Their homes in the ground.
   [Refrain 1]

10. And in that place
    Some people saw
    More prairie dogs
    Than you ever did see.
    Yes, the people said,
    "Let's save this place."
    And the big birds soared,
    And the owls burrowed,
    And the prairie dogs built
    Their homes in the ground.
    [Refrain 1]

11. And then one night
    There came some ferrets,
    The ones that crept
    On the softest feet.
    Yes, the people brought
    The ferrets back.
    And the ferrets crept,
    And the big birds soared,
    And the owls burrowed,
    And the prairie dogs built
    Their homes in the ground.
    [Refrain 1]

12. And then one day
    There came some bison,
    The ones that grazed
    And stomped their hooves.
    Yes, the people brought back
    Bison too.
    And the bison grazed,
    And the ferrets crept,
    And the big birds soared,
    And the owls burrowed,
    And the prairie dogs built
    Their homes in the ground.
    And the prairie dogs jumped
    and yipped, *"WEE-OO!"*
    [Refrain 1]

More Prairie Dog Facts

- Prairie dogs get their name from their alarm calls. Early explorers of the western United States thought the calls sounded like dogs barking.

- The five species of prairie dogs are: black-tailed prairie dogs, white-tailed prairie dogs, Gunnison's prairie dogs, Utah prairie dogs, and Mexican prairie dogs. All species of prairie dogs are now rare, and Utah and Mexican prairie dogs are threatened or endangered.

- A difference among species of prairie dogs is the color of their tails. Black-tailed and Mexican prairie dogs have long, black-tipped tails. Both kinds do jump-yips and do not hibernate. The other species have shorter tails that are white or gray at the tips. They do not jump-yip, and they do hibernate.

- A prairie dog will grow to be 12 to 17 inches (30.5 to 43 centimeters) tall and will weigh between 1 and 3 pounds (0.45 and 1.4 kilograms), depending on its species.

- Prairie dogs originally lived in southern Saskatchewan, Canada; Montana, North Dakota, South Dakota, Wyoming, Colorado, Nebraska, Kansas, Oklahoma, Texas, Arizona, New Mexico, and Utah in the United States; and Coahuila, Nuevo León, Zacatecas, and San Luis Potosí in northern Mexico. The Mexican prairie dog has disappeared from Zacatecas. Prairie dogs can still be found in parts of the other places.

- Prairie dogs "talk" to one another with many different sounds. They bark, yip, chatter, chirp, and make other noises. One scientist found that the sounds describe exactly what the prairie dog sees. For example, a prairie dog makes different sounds when it sees a dog or a coyote.

- A prairie dog family is called a coterie.

- Prairie dogs have one litter, or set of babies, a year. A litter usually consists of three to five pups.

- A prairie dog lives an average of three to four years in the wild.

- A black-tailed prairie dog town can have from one family to many thousands of prairie dogs.

- Prairie dogs mostly eat grasses but will also eat roots, shrubs, worms, and grasshoppers.

- When two members of a prairie dog family meet, they greet each other by touching their teeth in a "kiss."

Timeline of the Janos Grasslands

Prehistory: Grasslands cover central North America from southern Canada to northern Mexico. Billions of prairie dogs live in grass, along with burrowing owls, bison, golden eagles, black-footed ferrets, and many other animals.

In what is now Janos Biosphere Reserve, in Chihuahua, Mexico, live hunter-gatherers who leave behind petroglyphs and arrowheads.

Grasslands in Otero Mesa, New Mexico

Golden eagle

Black-tailed prairie dog

Black-footed ferret

Burrowing owl

Bison

1100s–1400s: People build city in northern Chihuahua that they later abandon, leaving behind ruins of the settlement, called Paquimé or Casas Grandes ("big houses").

Ruins of Paquimé

1565: Spanish explorers arrive.

1578: Town of Janos founded by Franciscan missionaries.

1689: Military outpost established to protect Janos from Apache raids, although Apaches still venture frequently into area.

1800s: Bison of northern Mexico hunted to near extinction.

Cattle ranches cover grasslands of North America from Manitoba, Canada, to Chihuahua, Mexico.

With government support, ranchers in United States begin killing prairie dogs by putting poison in their burrows.

1800s continued: Within 60 years, prairie dogs have been removed from 98 percent of their original territory. Prairie dogs' population shrinks from about 30 billion animals to 1 to 2 million. Animals, such as black-footed ferrets, that depend on prairie dogs as food also die off.

In parts of Mexico and southwestern United States, grasslands transform into desert; mesquite push their deep roots into the earth, sucking up water.

1892–1894: Major Edgar A. Mearns, army surgeon researching plants and animals for United States government along US–Mexico border, finds town of millions of prairie dogs in Chihuahua.

1988: Biologist Gerardo Ceballos drives with his wife, Guadalupe, through Chihuahua for first time and discovers extensive Janos grasslands. There are prairie dogs, he later says, "all the way to the horizon."

Gerardo Ceballos

Cattle grazing in prairie grass

1990s: Overgrazing by cattle and intensive land use for farming cause changes in Janos grasslands, including loss of soil and invasion of mesquite. People who can no longer find grass to feed their cattle sell their land to large-scale farmers. Many prairie dog town areas become farmland.

1991: Dr. Ceballos and Institute of Ecology at National Autonomous University of Mexico begin first biological studies in Janos grasslands.

Janos grasslands

2001: Dr. Ceballos and other scientists, including Dr. Rurik List, reintroduce black-footed ferrets to Janos grasslands.

Ferret reintroduction team, from left to right: Gerardo Ceballos, Jesús Pacheco, Rurik List, Rodrigo Sierra-Corona, Eduardo Ponce

2002: Dr. Ceballos, Dr. List, and other individuals and groups begin process to include Janos Biosphere Reserve in Mexico's National System of Protected Areas.

2005: The Nature Conservancy buys Rancho El Uno, a 46,000-acre (18,616-hectare) cattle ranch. The renamed Reserva Rancho El Uno is dedicated to restoring and sustainably managing grasslands and raising public awareness of grassland protection.

Black-tailed prairie dog jump-yipping

2009, November: Herd of 23 bison from Wind Cave National Park in South Dakota donated to El Uno by US National Park Service. Bison arrive in grasslands by tractor-trailer.

Nélida Barajas and her children watching bison herd

2009, December: 1.3 million-acre (526,000-hectare) Janos Biosphere Reserve (JBR) formally declared by federal government of Mexico. About 13,000 people live within JBR's lands, including cattle ranchers and farmers.

2010, May: Uno, first El Uno bison calf bred in Mexico, born. Uno is a female.

Calf Uno with her mother

2015: Bison herd has grown to 77 animals.

Bison herd grazing, with prairie dog town in background

Glossary and Pronunciation Guide

biologist (bye-OL-uh-gist): scientist who studies living things

bison (BYE-suhn): large wild animal with short horns, a mane, and a hump on its back; North American bison are also called buffalo

black-footed ferret (BLAK-fut-ed FEHR-et): small animal with a long, thin, tan body and black legs and feet that is a member of the weasel family

burrow (BUHR-oh): underground hole or tunnel dug by an animal

burrowing owl (BUHR-oh-ing owl): small owl with brown spotted feathers and bright yellow eyes; lives in burrow made by other animals

Chihuahua (chi-WAH-wah): state in northern Mexico that shares a border with New Mexico and Texas in the United States

coterie (KOH-tuh-ree): prairie dog family living together in a burrow

desert (DEZ-urt): dry area that gets very little rain

ecosystem (EK-oh-sis-tem or EE-koh-sis-tem): all plants and animals that live together in a place, along with nonliving things such as sunlight, soil, and water

endangered (en-DAYN-jerd): very rare; used to describe an animal or a plant species that is in great danger of dying out

environmental scientist (en-VIE-ruhn-MEN-tuhl SYE-uhn-tist): person who studies the natural world and how to protect it

extinction (ehk-STINGK-shun): state that results when something, such as an animal or a plant species, has died out and disappeared from Earth

Gerardo Ceballos (shehr-AR-doh say-BAH-jhos): scientist and professor at Institute of Ecology at National Autonomous University of Mexico who has worked since 1988 to help people understand the importance of prairie dogs in grassland ecosystems

glacier (GLAY-sher): large sheet of ice that moves slowly down a slope or valley or spreads over a wide area of land

golden eagle (GOHL-den EE-guhl): large eagle with brown feathers and golden-colored feathers on the back of its head and neck

grasses (GRAHS-ehs): different kinds of grass plants

grassland (GRAHS-land): area of land covered with grasses and other plants

graze (grayz): to feed on grass growing in a field

hibernate (HYE-buhr-nate): to spend the winter in a kind of sleep

horizon (huh-RYE-zuhn): line where the sky seems to meet the land or sea

Janos (HAH-nohss): town in Chihuahua, Mexico

Janos Biosphere Reserve (HAH-nohss BYE-uh-sfeer ree-SURV): grassland ecosystem in northern Mexico that is protected by the Mexican government

keystone species (KEE-stohn SPEE-sheez): group of animals that is very important to an ecosystem; if a keystone species is removed from an ecosystem, the plants and animals change and many might disappear

litter (LIT-uhr): group of young animals born at the same time to one mother

manure (muh-NOO-ur): animal's solid waste matter

maze (mayz): complicated network of connected passages

mesquite (meh-SKEET or MES-keet): tree with hard wood, thorns, and very long roots

Necesitamos bisontes. (nay-say-sih-TAH-mohs bih-ZON-tehs): Spanish for "We need bison."

Nélida Barajas (NEH-lih-dah bahr-AH-yahz): coordinator from 2007–2009 for The Nature Conservancy's Janos Grasslands project; played a role in early efforts to bring bison back to the grasslands

nitrogen (NYE-treh-jehn): gas that is part of Earth's air; nitrogen is found in the tissues of plants and animals

owlet (OU-let): young owl

Paquimé/Casas Grandes (PAK-ih-may/cah-SAZ GRAND-dez): ruins of a city in Chihuahua, Mexico, where people lived from the 1100s to the 1400s; Casas Grandes means "big houses" in Spanish

petroglyph (PEH-truh-glif): carving in a rock

prairie (PRAIR-ee): large, flat area of grassland

prairie dog (PRAIR-ee dog): small, furry, burrowing animal that is a member of the squirrel family

prairie dog complex (PRAIR-ee dog KOM-pleks): group of prairie dog towns located close enough together for a black-footed ferret to travel among them

predator (PRED-uh-tur): animal that hunts other animals for food

prey (pray): animal that is hunted by other animals for food

Reserva Rancho El Uno (reh-SERV-ah RAHN-choh el OO-noh): El Uno Ranch Reserve; *El uno* means "the one" or "the number one" in Spanish

Rurik List (RUHR-ik list): scientist and professor who studies the ecology and conservation of animals, including the Janos prairie dogs, ferrets, and bison

species (SPEE-sheez): group of plants or animals that are very similar and can produce young together

survive (sur-VIYVE): to stay alive

The Nature Conservancy (thuh NAY-chur kuhn-SER-vuhn-see): international nonprofit organization that works to protect nature around the world

threatened (THRET-nd): likely to be close to dying out at some time in the future; often used to describe an animal or a plant species that is in danger of dying out

town (toun): group of connected black-tailed prairie dog burrows

wingspan (WING-span): distance between the tips of a bird's outstretched wings

yip (yip): to make a high, fast, sharp noise or bark

Authors' Sources

Abumrad, Jad, and Robert Krulwich. "New Language Discovered: Prairiedogese." NPR Radiolab, January 20, 2011. http://www.npr.org/2011/01/20/132650631/new-language-discovered-prairiedogese.

Allred, Kelly W. *A Field Guide to the Grasses of New Mexico*, 3rd ed. Las Cruces, NM: New Mexico State University Agricultural Experiment Station, 2005.

Aschwanden, Christie. "Learning to Live With Prairie Dogs." National Wildlife Federation, April 1, 2001. http://www.nwf.org/news-and-magazines/national-wildlife/animals/archives/2001/learning-to-live-with-prairie-dogs.aspx.

Bard, Dario. "Black-Footed Ferrets Return to Mexico." *Endangered Species Bulletin* 27, no. 2 (March–June 2002): 36–37. http://www.fws.gov/endangered/bulletin/2002/03-06/36-37.pdf.

"Black-Footed Ferret." Utah Division of Wildlife Resources. Wildlife Notebook Series, no. 8 (June 2003). https://wildlife.utah.gov/publications/pdf/2010_black-footed_ferret.pdf.

Boudreaux, Yvonne. "Prairie Dogs: Wilderness Without Wildlife Is Just Scenery." New Mexico Wilderness Alliance, June 1, 2009. http://www.nmwild.org/2009/news/prairie-dogs/.

Ceballos, Gerardo, Ana Davidson, Rurik List, Jesús Pacheco, Patricia Manzano-Fischer, Georgina Santos-Barrera, and Juan Cruzado. "Rapid Decline of a Grassland System and Its Ecological and Conservation Implications." *PLoS ONE* 5, no. 1 (January 6, 2010). http://journals.plos.org/plosone/article?id=10.1371/journal.pone.0008562.

———, Eric Mellink, and Louise R. Hanebury. "Distribution and Conservation Status of Prairie Dogs *Cynomys Mexicanus* and *Cynomys Ludovicianus* in Mexico." *Biological Conservation* 63 (1993): 105–112.

——— and Jesús Pacheco. "The Prairie Dogs of Chihuahua: Their Biological Importance and Conservation." *Voices of Mexico* 54 (2001): 106–109.

"Chihuahuan Desert Lab Manual: Prairie Dogs." US National Park Service. http://www.nps.gov/cave/forteachers/upload/p3protocol.pdf.

"Conserving the Burrowing Owl." Defenders of Wildlife. http://www.defenders.org/sites/default/files/publications/conserving_the_burrowing_owl.pdf.

Ferris, Christiana. "Mexico: Janos Biosphere Reserve." The Nature Conservancy. http://www.nature.org/ourinitiatives/regions/northamerica/mexico/explore/biosphere-reserve-protects-mexicos-grasslands-for-the-first-time.xml.

"First Bison Conceived at El Uno." The Nature Conservancy. http://www.nature.org/ourinitiatives/regions/northamerica/mexico/explore/first-bison-conceived-at-el-uno.xml.

Griffin-Pierce, Trudy. *The Encyclopedia of Native America*. New York: Viking, 1995.

"Hampshire Folk Songs: Dr. Gardiner's Quest and the Result." *Hampshire Observer*, October 23, 1909. http://www.forest-tracks.co.uk/hampshirevoices/media/23.10.09_Quest%26Result_HO.pdf.

Hare, James F., Kevin L. Campbell, and Robert W. Senkiw. "Catch the Wave: Prairie Dogs Assess Neighbours' Awareness Using Contagious Displays." Proceedings B, The Royal Society, January 8, 2014. http://rspb.royalsocietypublishing.org/content/281/1777/20132153.

Jackson, Lora. *Prehistoric Indians of the El Paso Area*. El Paso, TX: El Paso Museum of Archaeology, 2005.

Johnsgard, Paul A. "The Howdy Owl and the Prairie Dog." *Birding* (January–February 2006): 40–44.

Kersten, Jason. "Welcome to El Uno." *Nature Conservancy* 61, no. 4 (Winter 2011).

Kocherga, Angela. "U.S., Mexico team up to bring wild bison back home on range." Video, 2:21. Posted by KENS 5 San Antonio, November 18, 2012, updated November 23, 2012. http://www.kens5.com/videos/news/2014/06/25/10314634/.

List, Rurik, Jesús Pacheco, Eduardo Ponce, Rodrigo Sierra-Corona, and Gerardo Ceballos. "The Janos Biosphere Reserve, Northern Mexico." *International Journal of Wilderness* 16, no. 2 (August 2010): 35–41.

Martinez-Estévez, Lourdes, Patricia Balvanera, Jesús Pacheco, and Gerardo Ceballos. "Prairie Dog Decline Reduces the Supply of Ecosystem Services and Leads to Desertification of Semiarid Grasslands." *PLoS ONE* 8, no. 10 (October 9, 2013). http://journals.plos.org/plosone/article?id=10.1371/journal.pone.0075229.

Palmquist, Darci. "Mexico: A Bison Homecoming." The Nature Conservancy, November 2009. http://www.nature.org/ourinitiatives/regions/northamerica/mexico/explore/bison-homecoming.xml.

"Prairie Dog." National Geographic. http://animals.nationalgeographic.com/animals/mammals/prairie-dog/.

"Prairie Dogs and Soil Impacts." Great Plains Restoration Council (GPRC). http://gprc.org/research/prairie-dogs-the-truth/prairie-dogs-and-soil-impacts/#.VLlIV1qvGoo.

"Prairie Grasslands." GlobalChange.gov/US Global Change Research Program. http://www.globalchange.gov/browse/educators/wildlife-wildlands-toolkit/eco-regions/grassland.

Rosmarino, Nicole. "Prairie Dogs Are a Keystone Species of the Great Plains." Southern Plains Land Trust. Fort Worth, TX: Great Plains Restoration Council, 2014.

Shapiro, Ari Daniel. "Can Prairie Dogs Save Mexico's Prairie From the Desert?" Interview with Gerardo Ceballos, Living on Earth, January 25, 2013. http://www.loe.org/shows/segments.html?programID=13-P13-00004&segmentID=8.

Sierra-Corona, Rodrigo, Ana Davidson, Ed L. Fredrickson, Hugo Luna-Soria, Humberto Suzan-Azpiri, Eduardo Ponce-Guevara, and Gerardo Ceballos. "Black-Tailed Prairie Dogs, Cattle, and the Conservation of North America's Arid Grasslands." *PLoS ONE* 10, no. 3 (March 11, 2015). http://journals.plos.org/plosone/article?id=10.1371/journal.pone.0118602.

Slobodchikoff, C. N., Bianca S. Perla, and Jennifer L. Verdolin. *Prairie Dogs: Communication and Community in an Animal Society*. Cambridge, MA: Harvard University Press, 2009.

Ulev, Elena. "*Cynomys ludovicianus*." Fire Effects Information System (FEIS). US Department of Agriculture Forest Service, Rocky Mountain Research Station, 2007. http://www.fs.fed.us/database/feis/animals/mammal/cylu/all.html.

Zielinski, Sarah. "Eliminating Prairie Dogs Can Lead to Desertification." *Science News*, October 17, 2013. https://www.sciencenews.org/blog/wild-things/eliminating-prairie-dogs-can-lead-desertification.